MEET JUDY SHEINDLIN

Behind the Robes – The Candid Biography of America's Favorite Judge

EVELYN FORD

Meet Judy Sheindlin

Copyright © 2024 by Evelyn Ford

All rights reserved. No part of this publication may be reproduced, distributed, or transmitted in any form or by any means, including photocopying, recording, or other electronic or mechanical methods, without the prior written permission of the publisher, except in the case of brief quotations embodied in critical reviews and certain other noncommercial uses permitted by copyright law.

CONTENTS

Introduction..1
Chapter 1: Early Years............................3
   Childhood in Brooklyn........................3
   Family Influences................................5
   Educational Journey...........................7
Chapter 2: The Legal Odyssey Begins....9
   Law School Years................................9
   Early Legal Career.............................10
   Judicial Aspirations..........................11
Chapter 3: The Rise to Fame...............13
   The Judge Judy Phenomenon....................13
   The Making of a TV Icon......................14
   Behind the Scenes.............................16
Chapter 4: Judy's Legal Legacy...........19
   Landmark Cases................................19
   Judicial Philosophy..........................24
   Impact on American Legal Culture...........26
Chapter 5: Personal Life Revealed.......29
   Marriage and Family..........................29
   Balancing Fame and Privacy...................31
   Candid Moments...............................32
   Hobbies and Interests........................35
   Relationship with Children and

Grandchildren..37
Influence and Support................................40
Chapter 6: Transition to New Ventures... 43
Judy Justice Unveiled................................43
Expanding the Legal Empire.....................45
Beyond the Bench..46
Chapter 7: The Public Persona............ 49
Media Appearances and Personal Opinions. 49
Influential Figures and Friends..................53
Judy's Impact on Pop Culture....................56
Chapter 8: Challenges and Triumphs.. 59
Navigating Controversies..........................59
Legal Battles Off-Screen............................63
Awards and Honors....................................67
Chapter 9: Legacy and Future.............. 71
Impact on the Legal System......................71
Enduring Popularity...................................73
Future Ventures and Contributions..........74
Conclusion.. 76

Introduction

Judy Sheindlin is more than just a judge. She is a cultural phenomenon and a media icon nd a legal legend. For 25 years and she presided over the top rated court show Judge Judy and where she dispensed justice and wisdom with her trademark wit and candor. Millions of viewers tuned in every day to watch her arbitrate small claims cases often with hilarious and memorable results. But behind the TV persona there is a remarkable woman who rose from humble beginnings to become one of the most influential and respected figures in the American legal system. In this biography and we will explore the life and career of Judy Sheindlin from her childhood in Brooklyn to her new venture Judy Justice. We will discover how she became America's beloved judge and why she is still unstoppable.

This is a biography of Judy Sheindlin the woman behind the gavel. She is a judge and a TV star and a cultural icon. She is known for her sharp wit and her tough justice and her catchy phrases. She is also a wife and a mother and a grandmother. She is Judge Judy.

Chapter 1: Early Years

Childhood in Brooklyn

Judy Sheindlin was born on October 21 and 1942 in Brooklyn, New York. She was the second child of Murray and Ethel Blum who were both Jewish immigrants from Germany and Russia and respectively. Judy grew up in a modest apartment in the Flatbush neighborhood and where she attended public schools. She was a bright and curious child who loved to read and write. She also developed a strong sense of justice and fairness which she attributed to her father who was a dentist and a respected member of the community. Judy often accompanied him to his office where she observed his interactions with his patients and learned the value of honesty and hard work.

Judy's childhood in Brooklyn was full of challenges and opportunities. She lived in a crowded and diverse neighborhood and where she learned to interact with people from different backgrounds and cultures. She also faced discrimination and prejudice as a Jewish girl in a predominantly Christian society. She recalled being called names and having rocks thrown at her by some of her classmates. Despite these hardships Judy did not let them affect her self esteem or her dreams. She was always eager to learn new things and to express her opinions. She enjoyed reading books especially biographies of famous people and writing stories and poems. She also participated in various extracurricular activities such as drama club, debate team and student council.

Family Influences

Judy's family was a major influence on her personality and career choices. Her parents were supportive and encouraging of her ambitions and instilled in her a sense of confidence and independence. Her mother Ethel was an office manager who handled the finances and household affairs. She was a practical and sensible woman who taught Judy how to be organized and efficient. Her father Murray was a warm and witty man and who inspired Judy with his stories and jokes. He also exposed her to the world of law and politics and by taking her to the library and the courthouse and the voting booth. Judy admired her father's integrity and compassion and wanted to follow in his footsteps as a professional and a leader.

Judy also had a close relationship with her siblings David, Marilyn and Steven. They often played together and shared their interests and supported each other. Judy was especially close to her older brother David who was also interested in law and politics. They would often discuss current events and debate various issues. David later became a lawyer and a judge and Judy credited him as one of her mentors and role models.

Educational Journey

Judy's educational journey was marked by excellence and achievement. She graduated from James Madison High School in Brooklyn in 1961 and where she was the editor of the school newspaper. She then enrolled at American University in Washington D.C. where she majored in government. She was the only woman in her class of 126 students and graduated with a Bachelor of Arts degree in 1963. She then pursued her law degree at New York Law School where she was again the only woman in her class. She graduated with a Juris Doctor degree in 1965 and passed the New York state bar examination the same year. Judy was determined to succeed in a male dominated field and proved herself to be a capable and competent lawyer.

Judy's education did not stop after she became a lawyer. She continued to learn and improve her skills throughout her career. She attended various seminars and workshops and conferences on topics related to family law and juvenile justice and arbitration. She also read books and articles on legal issues and psychology and sociology and philosophy. She was always curious and open minded and willing to challenge herself and others. She once said "I love the law. I love learning new things. I think that's what keeps you young."

Chapter 2: The Legal Odyssey Begins

Law School Years

Judy Sheindlin's law school years were challenging and rewarding. She enrolled at New York Law School in 1963 after graduating from American University with a degree in government. She was the only woman in her class of 126 students and faced sexism and discrimination from some of her professors and classmates. She recalled one incident where her advisor asked her why she was taking the seat of a man who would use his law degree to make a living. Sheindlin did not let these obstacles deter her from pursuing her passion for law. She studied hard and participated in moot court competitions and earned the respect of her peers. She graduated with a Juris Doctor degree in 1965 and passed the New York state bar examination afterwards.

Early Legal Career

Judy Sheindlin's early legal career was diverse and dynamic. She started as a corporate lawyer for a cosmetics firm but soon realized that she was not interested in the business side of law. She left the firm after two years to raise her two children, Jamie and Adam with her first husband Ronald Levy. In 1972, she became a prosecutor in the New York family court system after hearing about the job from a friend. She found her calling in the family court, where she handled cases involving child abuse and domestic violence and juvenile offenders. She was known for her tough and compassionate approach and as well as her ability to cut through the lies and excuses of the parties involved. She once said "I have a very strong sense of right and wrong. It's not hard to figure out who the good guys are and who the bad guys are."

Judicial Aspirations

Judy Sheindlin's judicial aspirations were inspired by her father who was a dentist and a civic leader. She admired his honesty and integrity and and wanted to follow in his footsteps as a professional and a leader. She also had a close relationship with her older brother and David and who was also a lawyer and a judge. They shared a common interest in law and politics and often discussed and debated different issues. David was one of her mentors and role models. Sheindlin's ambition and attitude caught the attention of New York mayor Ed Koch and who appointed her as a criminal court judge in 1982. She was thrilled to receive the opportunity and said "I wanted to be a judge since I was a little girl. I always had an innate sense of what was fair." Four years later, she was promoted to a supervising judge in the family court's Manhattan division where she oversaw the work of 46 judges and 300 support staff. She earned a reputation as a tough and efficient New York City judge who did not tolerate any nonsense or delays in her courtroom.

Chapter 3: The Rise to Fame

The Judge Judy Phenomenon

Judy Sheindlin's rise to fame began in 1993 when she was featured on the TV newsmagazine show 60 Minutes. The segment showcased her tough and witty style as a family court judge and attracted the attention of millions of viewers. She was approached by TV producers who offered her a chance to star in her own courtroom show similar to The People's Court. She accepted the offer and Judge Judy was born. The show debuted in 1996 and was an immediate hit in large part because of Sheindlin's quick and incisive rulings and brusque and no nonsense approach. She became known for her catchphrases like "Don't pee on my leg and tell me it is rainin'" and "Beauty fades and dumb is forever" and "I am speaking!". She also became known for her compassion and empathy for the victims of injustice and especially children and women. Judge Judy soon became the top rated court show in syndication and one of the most watched shows on daytime TV.

The Making of a TV Icon

Judy Sheindlin's success as a TV personality was not only based on her charisma and talent and but also on her hard work and professionalism. She worked closely with her longtime executive producer and director Randy Douthit and co executive producer Amy Freisleben who helped her create and maintain a high quality and entertaining show. She also had a loyal and supportive staff including her bailiff Petri Hawkins Byrd who was her former court officer in New York and her court reporter Whitney Kumar who joined the show in 2021. She also had a close relationship with her husband Jerry Sheindlin who was also a lawyer and a judge who briefly presided over The People's Court from 1999 to 2001. Sheindlin was involved in every aspect of the show from selecting the cases to editing the episodes. She was also very meticulous and punctual and expected the same from everyone else. She once said "I am a perfectionist. I like things done a certain way. I think that's what makes the show successful."

Behind the Scenes

Judy Sheindlin's show was not a real court but an arbitration based program that resolved real cases from small claims court. The disputing parties agreed to appear on the show and abide by Sheindlin's decision which was final and binding. They also received an appearance fee and a judgment fee depending on the outcome of the case. The show was filmed in Los Angeles where Sheindlin had a second home. She flew there every other week to tape the episodes, usually 10 cases a day for two or three days. The show was known for its fast pace and tight schedule which suited Sheindlin's personality. She did not like to waste time or tolerate any nonsense or delays in her courtroom. She also did not like to rehearse or prepare for the cases beforehand. She preferred to rely on her instincts and experience and to react spontaneously to the parties and the evidence. She said "I don't like to know anything about the litigants before I meet them. I like to be surprised. I think that's what makes the show interesting."

Meet Judy Sheindlin

Chapter 4: Judy's Legal Legacy

Landmark Cases

Judy Sheindlin's legal legacy includes some landmark cases that she handled as a judge or an arbitrator. Some of these cases involved controversial or complex issues such as child custody and parental rights, wrongful death, defamation and fraud. Some of these cases also had significant social or legal implications like setting precedents and changing laws or influencing public opinion. Here are some of Sheindlin's landmark cases:

- In 1988, Sheindlin presided over the case of Gregory Kingsley and a

12 year old boy who wanted to sever his ties with his biological mother and be adopted by his foster parents. Sheindlin granted his wish making him the first child in the U.S. to legally divorce his parents. The case sparked a national debate on the rights of children and parents and was later made into a TV movie, A Place to Be Loved and starring Sheindlin as herself.

- In 1995, Sheindlin ruled in favor of a woman who sued her ex husband for infecting her with HIV. She awarded the woman $12.5 million in damages which is the largest amount ever granted in a matrimonial case in New York. Sheindlin said that the man had committed "a heinous act of nondisclosure" and that he deserved "to be punished to the fullest extent of the law".

- In 2017 Sheindlin arbitrated a dispute between two dog owners over the ownership of a poodle named Baby Boy. She decided the case by letting the dog loose in the courtroom and observing which owner he ran to. The dog ran to the plaintiff who claimed that he had bought the dog from someone on the street while the defendant claimed that the dog was hers and that he had been stolen from her. Sheindlin ruled that the plaintiff was the rightful owner of the dog saying that "it was clear that the dog loved the plaintiff".
- In 2019, Sheindlin arbitrated a dispute between two former

business partners over the ownership of a rare and valuable coin collection. She decided the case by ordering an expert appraisal of the coins which revealed that they were worth over $200,000. She then ruled that the plaintiff who had invested in the coins was entitled to half of their value while the defendant who had stored and maintained the coins was entitled to the other half. She also ordered the defendant to pay the plaintiff $5,000 in damages for withholding the coins from him.

- In 2020, Sheindlin presided over the case of a woman who sued her ex boyfriend for stealing her dog and selling it to another woman. She decided the case by examining the evidence which included a receipt, a microchip and a text message. She concluded that the plaintiff was the rightful owner of the dog and ordered the defendant to return the dog to her and pay her $2,500 in damages. She also scolded the defendant for his dishonest and cruel behavior saying that "you don't sell someone's dog. That's despicable".

- In 2021, Sheindlin arbitrated a dispute between two neighbors over the damage caused by a fallen tree. She decided the case by inspecting the photos and videos of the scene which showed that the tree had fallen from the defendant's property onto the plaintiff's fence and car. She determined that the defendant was liable for the damage and ordered him to pay the plaintiff $6,000 in damages. She also advised the defendant to trim his trees regularly saying that "you have a responsibility to maintain your property and especially when it affects your neighbor's property".

Judicial Philosophy

Judy Sheindlin's judicial philosophy is based on her belief in the rule of law and the pursuit of justice and the protection of the innocent. She has described herself as a "strict constructionist" meaning that she interprets the law "as it is written and not as I would like it to be". She has also said that she follows the principles of "common sense, fairness and honesty" in her decisions. She has expressed her disdain for "legal mumbo jumbo" and "technicalities" that often obscure the truth or delay the resolution of cases. She has also criticized some aspects of the legal system such as the excessive use of plea bargains and the leniency of some judges and the inefficiency of some courts.

Sheindlin's judicial philosophy is also influenced by her experience as a family court judge and a prosecutor. She has a special concern for the welfare of children and women who are often the victims of abuse and neglect and or violence. She has advocated for the rights of children to have a safe and loving environment and for the responsibility of parents to provide for their children's needs. She has also supported the empowerment of women to stand up for themselves to pursue their goals. She has said that "the message that I try to convey to women is that they have to be able to take care of themselves".

Impact on American Legal Culture

Judy Sheindlin's impact on American legal culture is evident in her popularity and influence and recognition. She has been widely praised for her contribution to the public understanding of the law and the promotion of alternative dispute resolution and the inspiration of future generations of lawyers and judges.

She has been the host of the top rated court show in syndication and Judge Judy for 25 seasons reaching millions of viewers every day. She has also launched a new show Judy Justice on IMDb TV (now Amazon Freevee) in 2021.

She has been the recipient of numerous awards and honors such as the Lifetime Achievement Emmy Award in 2019 and the Guinness World Record for the longest serving television arbitrator in 2015 and and the Gracie Allen Tribute Award in 2014.

She has been the subject of several documentaries like the Judge Judy: Justice Served (2007) and Judge Judy Primetime (2014) and Judy Justice: The Makin' of a TV Icon (2021).

She has been the inspiration and mentor for many aspiring and practicing lawyers and judges especially women and minorities. She has also supported various educational and charitable causes such as the Her Honor Mentoring Program, the Judge Judy Sheindlin Scholarship and the Judge Judy Sheindlin Reading Room.

Chapter 5: Personal Life Revealed

Marriage and Family

Judy Sheindlin's personal life has been marked by love, loss and resilience. She has been married three times and has five children and 13 grandchildren. Her first husband was Ronald Levy, a lawyer whom she met at a bar in Washington D.C. They got married in 1964 and had two children Jamie and Adam. They got divorced in 1976 after 12 years of marriage. Her second husband was Jerry Sheindlin also a lawyer and a judge whom she met at a party in New York. They got married in 1977 and had three children Gregory, Jonathan and Nicole. They got divorced in 1990 after

13 years of marriage but remarried a year later. They have been together ever since. Sheindlin has described Jerry as her "best friend and soulmate" and and said that "he makes me laugh every day".

Sheindlin's family is very important to her and she tries to spend as much time as possible with them. She often hosts family gatherings at her homes in Connecticut, Florida and Wyoming where she enjoys cooking and playing games and reading to her grandchildren. She also travels with her family to various destinations and such as Israel and Italy and Australia. She is very proud of her children and grandchildren who have pursued careers in law, medicine education and entertainment.

Balancing Fame and Privacy

Judy Sheindlin's fame and privacy have been in constant tension throughout her career. She has been one of the most recognizable and popular figures on TV and but she has also been one of the most private and guarded. She has said that "I don't like being a celebrity. I like being a judge. I like being a person who has a job that I love". She has also said that "I don't want to be bothered when I am not working. I don't want to be recognized. I don't want to be photographed. I don't want to be interviewed".

Sheindlin has tried to maintain a low profile and avoid the spotlight when she is not on the air. She rarely gives interviews or attends public events and prefers to stay at home or go to places where she is not recognized. She also values her security and safety and has hired bodyguards and installed surveillance cameras at her homes. She has also been involved in several lawsuits and disputes with the media and the paparazzi and the public over issues such as defamation and invasion of privacy and harassment.

Candid Moments

Judy Sheindlin's candid moments have revealed her human and humorous side and as well as her opinions and passions. She has often shared stories and anecdotes from her personal and professional life both on and off the screen. She has also expressed her views and feelings on various topics and such as politics, religion, education and health. Some of her candid moments are:

In 2007 she revealed that she had suffered a mini stroke which caused her to lose her vision temporarily. She said that the incident was a wake up call for her to take better care of herself and to appreciate life more.

In 2012 and she appeared on the TV show Katie hosted by Katie Couric and and surprised the audience by taking off her signature lace collar and revealing a tattoo on her chest. The tattoo was a gift from her husband Jerry for their 37th anniversary and it read "Jerry's Girl".

In 2016 she endorsed Michael Bloomberg for president saying that he was "the only adult in the room" and that he had "the experience and the intelligence and the temperament" to lead the country.

In 2018 she appeared on the TV show The Ellen DeGeneres Show and played a game of "Would You Rather" with Ellen DeGeneres. She chose George Clooney over Brad Pitt and Oprah Winfrey over Reese Witherspoon and Barack Obama over Donald Trump.

In 2020 she donated $4 million to the University of Southern California to create the Judy and Jerry Sheindlin Forum and a space for public debate and dialogue on campus. She said that the forum was "a gift to the future generations of students who will learn the value of civil discourse and the exchange of ideas".

Hobbies and Interests

Judy Sheindlin has a variety of hobbies and interests that she enjoys outside of her work. Some of these hobbies and interests are:

Gardening: Sheindlin loves to garden and grow flowers and vegetables and and herbs at her homes in Connecticut, Florida and Wyoming. She has said that gardening is "a relaxing and rewarding activity" and that "it gives me a sense of accomplishment and beauty".

Cooking: Sheindlin likes to cook and bake for her family and friends especially during holidays and special occasions. She has said that cooking is "a creative and fun way to express my love and gratitude" and that "I like to try new recipes and experiment with different flavors".

Traveling: Sheindlin likes to travel and explore new places and cultures with her husband Jerry, her children and grandchildren. She has once said that traveling is "an educational and adventurous experience" and that "I like to learn about the history, the people and the customs of different countries". She has visited various tourist destinations like Israel, Italy and Australia.

Reading: Sheindlin likes to read books and articles on various topics such as law and psychology, sociology and philosophy. She has said that reading is "a stimulating and enriching activity" and that "I like to expand my knowledge and challenge my mind". She also likes to read to her grandchildren and share her favorite stories with them.

Playing games: Sheindlin likes to play games and puzzles with her family and friends such as Scrabble and Sudoku and crossword puzzles. She has said that playing games is "a fun and competitive activity" and that "I like to test my skills and show off my vocabulary". She also likes to watch and play sports such as tennis, golf and skiing.

Relationship with Children and Grandchildren

Judy Sheindlin has a close and loving relationship with her children and grandchildren who have been a source of joy and pride for her. She has five children, two from her first marriage to Ronald Levy and three from her second marriage to Jerry Sheindlin. Her children are Jamie, Adam, Gregory, Jonathan and Nicole. She also has 13 grandchildren who range in age from toddlers to adults. She has said that her grandchildren are "the light of my life" and that "they make me happy every day".

Sheindlin has been a supportive and involved parent and grandparent and who has tried to balance her work and family life. She has said that she always made time for her children even when she was busy with her career. She has also said that she always encouraged her children to pursue their dreams and goals and to be independent and responsible. She has also said that she was tough on her children but not too tough and that she taught them the values of honesty, fairness and respect.

Sheindlin has also been a proud and delighted parent and grandparent who has celebrated and shared the achievements and milestones of her children and grandchildren. She has said that she is amazed and impressed by the accomplishments and talents of her children and grandchildren who have pursued various careers in law, medicine, education and entertainment. She loves to attend and host family gatherings and events like weddings, birthdays and holidays where she enjoys every moment with her grandchildren.

Influence and Support

Judy Sheindlin's children and grandchildren have also influenced and supported her in various ways both personally and professionally. Some of the ways that they have influenced and supported her are:

Her children have followed her footsteps and become lawyers and judges and which has made her proud and inspired. Her son Adam is the district attorney of Putnam County New York and her stepson Gregory is a judge in the Bronx Supreme Court. Her daughter Nicole is also a lawyer who works with her on the mentoring program, Her Honor Mentoring.

Her granddaughter Sarah Rose has joined her as a co star on her new show Judy Justice where she serves as a legal analyst. Sheindlin has praised her for her intelligence and professionalism and and said that "she is a chip off the old block".

Her children and grandchildren have given her feedback and advice on her shows and her books which has helped her improve and grow. She has said that her children and grandchildren are her "biggest critics and fans" and that they often watch her show, read her books and tell her what they think.

Her children and grandchildren have also given her love and comfort especially during difficult and challenging times. She has said that her children and grandchildren are her "rock and anchor" and that they always support and encourage her and and make her feel better.

Chapter 6: Transition to New Ventures

Judy Justice Unveiled

Judy Sheindlin's transition to new ventures began in 2020 when she announced that she would end her long running show Judge Judy after 25 seasons. She said that she wanted to move on to a new challenge and a new platform and that she was not ready to retire. She revealed that she had signed a deal with Amazon Freevee a free streaming service to launch a new show called Judy Justice. She said that the new show would be similar to Judge Judy but with some differences such as a new set and a new format and a new team. She said that the new show would be a little bit more personal and a little bit more behind the scenes.

Judy Justice premiered on November 1 2021 and was an instant success attracting millions of viewers and rare reviews. Sheindlin returned to her role as an arbitrator resolving real cases from small claims court. She was joined by her granddaughter Sarah Rose who served as a legal analyst and Kevin Rasco who served as a bailiff. She also had a panel of three rotating judges who offered their opinions and insights on the cases. Sheindlin said that the new show was "a fresh and exciting way to deliver justice".

Expanding the Legal Empire

Judy Sheindlin's new ventures also included expanding her legal empire beyond the courtroom. She continued to produce and oversee her other courtroom show Hot Bench which she created in 2014. The show featured three judges who heard and decided cases together and often had heated debates and disagreements. Sheindlin said that the show was "a dynamic and innovative twist on the traditional court show".

She also launched a new show Tribunal in 2021 which was a spin off of Judy Justice. The show featured the three judges from Judy Justice who presided over more complex and controversial cases such as civil rights, constitutional law and international law. The show also had a jury of 12 people and who voted on the verdicts. Sheindlin said that the show was "a groundbreaking and educational show that tackled the most important and relevant issues of our time".

Beyond the Bench

Judy Sheindlin's new ventures also extended beyond the legal realm into other fields and interests. She continued to write and publish books and such as Judy's Rules for Life (2022) which was a collection of her advice and wisdom on various topics and such as love, money, health and happiness.

She also pursued her passion for philanthropy and education and donated millions of dollars to various causes and institutions. She donated $4 million to the University of Southern California her alma mater to create the Judy and Jerry Sheindlin Forum, a space for public debate and dialogue on campus. She also donated $2 million to the New York Law School where she graduated from, to establish the Judge Judy Sheindlin Center for Family Law and Policy. She also supported various educational and charitable programs and such as the Her Honor Mentoring Program and the Judge Judy Sheindlin Scholarship and the Judge Judy Sheindlin Reading Room.

Meet Judy Sheindlin

Chapter 7: The Public Persona

Media Appearances and Personal Opinions

Judy Sheindlin's public persona has been shaped by her numerous media appearances both on and off the screen. She has been featured on various TV shows and magazines and podcasts and documentaries where she has shared her opinions, stories and insights on various topics. She has also been the recipient of many awards and honors and such as the Lifetime Achievement Emmy Award in 2019 and the Guinness World Record for the longest serving television arbitrator in

2015 and the Gracie Allen Tribute Award in 2014.

Some of her notable media appearances are given below:

In 1993 and she was profiled on the TV news magazine show 60 Minutes and which showcased her tough and witty style as a family court judge and and attracted the attention of millions of viewers. This popular segment led to her TV deal with Judge Judy.

In 2016 she endorsed Michael Bloomberg for president and saying that he was "the only adult in the room" and that he had "the experience, the intelligence and the temperament" to lead the country.

In 2018 and she appeared on the TV show The Ellen DeGeneres Show and played a game of "Would You Rather" with Ellen DeGeneres. She chose George Clooney over Brad Pitt and Oprah Winfrey over Reese Witherspoon and Barack Obama over Donald Trump.

Judy Sheindlin has also expressed her opinions and views on current relevant issues such as the social justice movement and the 2024 presidential election.

She has supported the social justice movement which advocates for the rights and equality of marginalized groups such as racial minorities, women and LGBTQ+ people. She has said that she believes in the principles of "liberty and justice for all" and that she respects and celebrates the diversity and dignity of all people. She has also said that she condemns and opposes any form of discrimination, oppression or violence against any group or individual.

She has endorsed Nikki Haley and the former governor of South Carolina and the former ambassador to the United Nations for the 2024 presidential election. She has praised Haley's intelligence, experience and character saying that she is "whip smart" and "principled" and "the future of this great nation". She has also said that she thinks Haley can "restore America" and "lead the country with common sense and honesty".

Influential Figures and Friends

Judy Sheindlin's public persona has also been influenced by her relationships with influential figures and friends in various fields and industries. She has been inspired and mentored by some of the most respected and accomplished people in the legal profession such as Judge Jane Bolin the first Black woman judge in the U.S. and Mayor Ed Koch who appointed her to the bench. She has also been supported and admired by some of the most famous talented people in the entertainment industry such as Bette Midler, Samuel L. Jackson, Florence Henderson and Joan Rivers.

Meet Judy Sheindlin

Her husband Jerry Sheindlin is also a lawyer and a judge who briefly presided over The People's Court from 1999 to 2001.

Judge Jane Bolin: She was the first Black woman judge in the U.S., who served on the New York City Domestic Relations Court from 1939 to 1978. She was a pioneer and a trailblazer in the field of law, who fought for racial and gender equality and justice. Sheindlin has said that she was inspired by Bolin's courage and integrity, and that she considered her as a role model and a mentor.

Mayor Ed Koch: He was the mayor of New York City from 1978 to 1989, who transformed and revitalized the city with his leadership and charisma. He was also a lawyer and a judge, who had a keen interest and involvement in the legal system. He appointed Sheindlin as a criminal-court judge in 1982, and promoted her to supervising judge in the family court's Manhattan division in 1986. Sheindlin has said that she was grateful and honored by Koch's trust and support, and that she learned a lot from his wisdom and vision.

Bette Midler: She is a singer, actress, and activist, who has won multiple awards and honors for her work in music, film, and television. She is also a fan and a friend of Sheindlin, who has watched her show for years. She has called her "a national treasure", and said that "she is the voice of reason in a world gone mad".

Samuel L. Jackson: He is an actor and producer, who has starred in many blockbuster movies and franchises, such as Pulp Fiction, The Avengers, and Star Wars. He is also a guest and a friend of Sheindlin, who has appeared on her show as a litigant. He has called her "the ultimate boss", and said that "she is the coolest person on the planet".

Judy's Impact on Pop Culture

Judy Sheindlin's public persona has had a tremendous impact on pop culture as she has become one of the most recognizable and beloved figures in the world. She has inspired and entertained millions of people with her show and her books and her quotes and her style. She has also influenced and shaped the public perception and understanding of the law and the court system and the role of the judge. She has been named one of the 100 most influential people in the world by Time magazine.

She has created a genre of courtroom shows which have become popular and profitable in the TV industry. She has also set the standard for quality and ratings as her show has been the top rated court show in syndication for 25 seasons and one of the most watched shows on daytime TV.

Meet Judy Sheindlin

Chapter 8: Challenges and Triumphs

Navigating Controversies

Judy Sheindlin's challenges and triumphs have not been limited to the courtroom. She has also faced and overcome various controversies and criticisms throughout her career. Some of these controversies and criticisms have involved her judicial style, her political views, her personal life, and her show's impact. Here are some examples of how Sheindlin has navigated controversies:

- She has defended her judicial style, which has been described as harsh, rude, and biased by some of her critics.

She has said that she is not a bully, but a realist, and that she does not tolerate nonsense, lies, or excuses. She has also said that she treats everyone equally, regardless of their race, gender, or background. She has argued that her style is effective and necessary, especially in the family court, where she dealt with serious and sensitive issues. She has said that her style is also entertaining and educational, and that it appeals to the viewers who want to see justice done.

- She has expressed her political views, which have been labeled as conservative by some of her critics. She has said that she is not a political person, but a common-sense person, and that she does not belong to any party or ideology. She has said that she supports the rule of law, the protection of the innocent, and the accountability of the guilty. She has also said that she is in favor of gun control, abortion rights, gay rights, and immigration reform. She has endorsed candidates from both parties, such as Michael Bloomberg and Joe Biden, based on their qualifications and character.

- She has dealt with her personal life, which has been scrutinized and speculated by some of the media and the public. She has said that she values her privacy and does not like to share her personal details with strangers. She has also said that she does not care about what others think of her, as long as she is happy and comfortable with herself. She has overcome various challenges in her personal life, such as divorce, health issues, and family conflicts. She has also enjoyed various achievements in her personal life, such as marriage, parenthood, and grandparenthood.

- She has responded to her show's impact, which has been praised and criticized by some of the legal experts and the public. She has said that she is proud of her show and its contribution to the public understanding of the law and the court system. She has also said that she is aware of her show's limitations and responsibilities, and that she does not claim to be a perfect or a representative judge. She has acknowledged that her show is not a real court, but a form of alternative dispute resolution, and that she does not follow the same rules and procedures as a real court. She has also emphasized that her show is not only a legal show, but also a human-interest show, and that she tries to balance the legal and the human aspects of each case.

Legal Battles Off-Screen

Judy Sheindlin's challenges and triumphs have also involved legal battles off-screen. She has been involved in several lawsuits and disputes with various parties, such as former colleagues, business partners, media outlets, and litigants. Some of these lawsuits and disputes have concerned issues such as contracts, profits, rights, defamation, privacy, and harassment. Here are some examples of Sheindlin's legal battles off-screen:

- She sued Richard Lawrence, a former talent agent who represented her in the early days of her show, and his company Rebel Entertainment Partners, for breach of contract and unjust enrichment. She claimed that Lawrence and Rebel had no right to receive profits from her show, as they had not performed any services or contributed any value to her show. She also claimed that Lawrence and Rebel had interfered with her deal with CBS, which bought the rights to her show's library for $95 million. Lawrence and Rebel countersued Sheindlin and CBS, alleging that the library sale was a sham transaction that deprived them of their rightful share of the profits. The lawsuits are still pending in court.

- She was sued by Patrice Jones, a woman who appeared as a plaintiff on her show, for emotional distress and false imprisonment. Jones claimed that Sheindlin had humiliated and berated her on national TV, and that the show's producers had coerced and manipulated her into signing a release form and participating in the show. She also claimed that the show's staff had detained her against her will and prevented her from leaving the studio. Sheindlin and the show's producers denied the allegations and moved to dismiss the lawsuit. The lawsuit was dismissed by the court.

- She was sued by Kaye Switzer, a former producer who worked with her on her show, for age discrimination and wrongful termination. Switzer claimed that Sheindlin had fired her because of her age, and that she had replaced her with a younger and less-experienced producer. She also claimed that Sheindlin had mistreated and harassed her, and that she had created a hostile and abusive work environment. Sheindlin and the show's producers denied the allegations and moved to dismiss the lawsuit. The lawsuit was settled out of court.

- She was sued by John Haymond, a personal injury lawyer who used clips from her show in his TV commercials, for unauthorized use of her image and trademark. She claimed that Haymond had violated her rights and damaged her reputation by associating her with his law firm without her consent. She also claimed that Haymond had ignored her cease-and-desist letters and continued to air the commercials. Haymond countersued Sheindlin, alleging that she had defamed him and his law firm by calling him a "chase lawyer" and a "tortfeasor" on her show. The lawsuits were settled out of court.

Awards and Honors

Judy Sheindlin's challenges and triumphs have also been recognized and celebrated by various awards and honors. She has received numerous accolades and distinctions from various organizations and institutions, such as the television industry, the legal profession, the media, and the academia. Some of these awards and honors have acknowledged her achievements and contributions in the fields of law, entertainment, education, and philanthropy. Here are some examples of Sheindlin's awards and honors:

- She received the Lifetime Achievement Emmy Award in 2019, for her exceptional and enduring contribution to the television medium. She was the first television arbitrator to receive this prestigious award, which was presented to her by Amy Poehler at the 46th Annual Daytime Emmy Awards. She also received four Daytime Emmy Awards for Outstanding Legal/Courtroom Program, three for Judge Judy and one for Judy Justice.

- She received the Guinness World Record for the longest-serving television arbitrator in 2015, for her 19 years of service on Judge Judy. She was presented with the certificate by her friend and fellow TV personality Larry King on his show Larry King Now. She also received the Guinness World Record for the highest-paid television host in 2018, for earning $147 million in the previous year.

- She received the Gracie Allen Tribute Award in 2014, for her positive and influential impact on the media landscape and society. She was honored by the Alliance for Women in Media Foundation at the 39th Annual Gracie Awards Gala. She also received the Brandon Tartikoff Legacy Award in 2013, for her extraordinary passion, leadership, and vision in the television industry. She was honored by the National Association of Television

Meet Judy Sheindlin

Program Executives at the 10th Annual Brandon Tartikoff Legacy Awards.

- She received a star on the Hollywood Walk of Fame in 2006, for her outstanding achievement in the field of television. She was inducted into the Walk of Fame by the Hollywood Chamber of Commerce at a ceremony attended by her family, friends, and fans. Her star is located at 7065 Hollywood Boulevard. She also received an honorary Doctor of Law degree in 2006, for her distinguished career and service in the field of law. She was conferred the degree by the University of Pennsylvania Law School at a commencement ceremony.

Chapter 9: Legacy and Future

Impact on the Legal System

Judy Sheindlin's legacy and future are closely tied to her impact on the legal system. She has been a pioneer and a leader in the field of law, both as a judge and as a television arbitrator. She has demonstrated her expertise and excellence in handling various types of cases, from family law to civil law. She has also shown her innovation and creativity in developing and promoting alternative dispute resolution, such as arbitration and mediation. She has said that her goal is to "make the law accessible and understandable to the people".

Sheindlin's impact on the legal system is also evident in her influence and inspiration on other lawyers and judges, especially women and minorities. She has been a role model and a mentor for many aspiring and practicing legal professionals, who have followed her footsteps and learned from her wisdom. She has also supported and encouraged various educational and professional programs and organizations, such as the New York Law School, the American Bar Association, and the National Association of Women Judges. She has said that she hopes to "leave a legacy of fairness, honesty, and integrity" in the legal system.

Enduring Popularity

Judy Sheindlin's legacy and future are also reflected in her enduring popularity. She has been one of the most successful and beloved figures in the television industry, as well as in the public eye. She has attracted and entertained millions of viewers and fans with her show, her books, her quotes, and her style. She has also received and appreciated numerous accolades and distinctions from various sources, such as the television industry, the media, and the academia. She has said that she is grateful and humbled by the recognition and support that she has received from the people.

Sheindlin's popularity is also manifested in her impact on pop culture. She has become a cultural icon and a household name, who has inspired and influenced various aspects of popular culture, such as language, humor, fashion, and art. She has also been featured and referenced in various forms of media and entertainment, such as movies, music, books, and games. She has said that she is amused and flattered by the attention and admiration that she has received from the pop culture.

Future Ventures and Contributions

Judy Sheindlin's legacy and future are also shaped by her future ventures and contributions. She has not stopped working and creating, even after ending her long-running show Judge Judy. She has launched a new show, Judy Justice, on Amazon Freevee, where she continues to arbitrate real cases and deliver justice. She has also expanded her legal empire, by producing and overseeing other courtroom shows, such as Hot Bench and Tribunal. She has said that she enjoys and challenges herself with new projects and platforms.

Sheindlin's future ventures and contributions are also driven by her passion and vision for philanthropy and education. She has donated millions of dollars to various causes and institutions, which we looked at in previous chapters. By all means, she aims to give back to the society and the future generations.

Conclusion

Judy Sheindlin's journey has been remarkable and inspiring. She has risen from humble beginnings to become one of the most influential and respected figures in the legal system and the television industry. She has overcome various challenges and controversies, and achieved numerous successes and honors. She has also made a lasting impact on the society and the culture, as well as on the lives of millions of people.

Sheindlin's journey is not over yet. She continues to work and create, to share and give back, to challenge and entertain. She is always looking for new opportunities and adventures, and never settles for anything less than excellence.

She is always true to herself and her values, and never afraid to speak her mind and stand her ground. She is the unstoppable Judge Judy, and she is not done yet.

Sheindlin's journey also offers many lessons and insights that we can learn from and apply to our own lives. Some of these lessons and insights are:

- Be honest and truthful. Sheindlin has always valued honesty and truthfulness, both in herself and in others. She has said that "if you tell the truth, you don't have to have a good memory" and that "if it doesn't make sense, it probably isn't true". She has also shown that honesty and truthfulness can lead to success and respect, as well as justice and fairness.

- Be responsible and self-reliant. Sheindlin has always advocated for personal responsibility and self-reliance, both in her work and in her life. She has said that "you have to be able to take care of yourself" and that "you are responsible for the choices that you make". She has also demonstrated that responsibility and self-reliance can lead to independence and empowerment, as well as happiness and fulfillment.

- Be confident and assertive. Sheindlin has always displayed confidence and assertiveness, both in her profession and in her personality. She has said that "I know who I am and what I can do" and that "I'm speaking!" . She has also proven that confidence and assertiveness can lead to recognition and influence, as well as admiration and inspiration.

Made in the USA
Monee, IL
07 October 2024